SCHOLASTIC

Comprehension Practice Ages 5–7

Revision & Practice

KS1 Years 1–2

Who?
What?
Where?
Story

Build confidence with targeted skills practice

Comprehension

Published in the UK by Scholastic, 2016

Scholastic Distribution Centre, Bosworth Avenue, Tournament Fields, Warwick, CV34 6UQ

Scholastic Ireland, 89E Lagan Road, Dublin Industrial Estate, Glasnevin, Dublin, D11 HP5F

SCHOLASTIC and associated logos are trademarks and/or registered trademarks of Scholastic Inc.

www.scholastic.co.uk

© 2016 Scholastic

13 14 15 16 17 18 19 20 3 4 5 6 7 8 9 0 1 2

A CIP catalogue record for this book is available from the British Library.

ISBN 978-1407-14178-7

Printed and bound by Bell and Bain Ltd, Glasgow

Paper made from wood grown in sustainable forests and other controlled sources.

Acknowledgements

The publishers gratefully acknowledge permission to reproduce the following copyright material: **Andersen Press Ltd** for permission to use an extract from *My Friend Nigel* by Jo Hodgkinson. © 2012, Jo Hodgkinson. (2012, Andersen Press Ltd). **Dorling Kindersley Ltd** for the use of the cover from *Seasons* by Marie Greenwood. © 2012, Dorling Kindersley Ltd. (2012, DK Publishing). **Egmont UK Ltd** for permission to use text and an illustration from *Shouty Arthur* by Angie Morgan. Text and illustration © 2014, Angie Morgan. (2014, Egmont UK Ltd). **Hachette UK** for the use of text and illustrations from *How to Babysit a Grandad* by Jean Reagan, illustrated by Lee Wildish. Text © 2013, Jean Reagan. Illustrations © 2013, Lee wildish. (2013, Hodder Children's Books); text and an illustration from *Once there was a Raindrop* by Judith Anderson and Mike Gordon. © 2009, Wayland. (2009, Wayland); text and illustrations from *Once There Was a Tadpole* by Judith Anderson and Mike Gordon. © 2009, Wayland. (2009, Wayland). **Oxford University Press** for permission to use an extract from *Hugh Shampoo* by Karen George. Text and illustrations © 2013, Karen George. (Oxford University Press, 2013). **Random House Children's Books** for permission to use text and an illustration from *Picnic* by John Burningham. © 2013, John Burningham. (2013, Jonathan Cape); text and illustrations from *Green Light for the Little Red Train* by Benedict Blathwayt. © 2002, Benedict Blathwayt. (2002, Hutchinson); text and illustrations from *My Big Shouting Day* by Rebecca Patterson. © 2012, Rebecca Patterson. (2012, Jonathan Cape); text and an illustration from *My Busy Being Bella Day* by Rebecca Patterson. © 2013, Rebecca Patterson. (2013, Jonathan Cape); text and illustrations from *Traction Man and the Beach Odyssey* by Mini Grey. © 2011, Mini Grey. (2011, Jonathan Cape). **Scholastic Children's Books** for permission to use text and illustrations from *How To Hide a Lion* by Helen Stephens. Text and illustrations © 2012, Helen Stephens. (2012, Alison Green Books). **Troika Books** for permission to use the poem 'Sally McDuff' and an illustration from *Blue Balloons and Rabbit Ears*. Text and illustration © 2014, Hilda Offen. (2014, Troika Books). **Kaye Umansky** for permission to use an extract from 'Ten Tubby Teddies' from *Nonsense Counting Rhymes*. Text © 1999, Kaye Umansky. (1999, Oxford University Press). **Walker Books Ltd** for permission to use the cover, a text extract and illustrations from *Nurse Clementine* by Simon James. Text and illustrations © 2013, Simon James. (2013, Walker Books Ltd); text and illustrations from *We're Going on a Bear Hunt* by Michael Rosen, illustrated by Helen Oxenbury. Text © 1989, Michael Rosen. Illustrations © 1989, Helen Oxenbury. (1989, Walker Books Ltd); text and illustrations from *Knuffle Bunny* by Mo Willems. Text and illustrations © 2005, Mo Willems. (2005, Walker Books Ltd); text and an illustration from *Baby Brains* by Simon James. Text and illustration © 2004, Simon James. (2004, Walker Books Ltd); text and an illustration from *One Tiny Turtle* by Nicola Davies, illustrated by Jane Chapman. Text © 2001, Nicola Davies. Illustrations © 2001, Jane Chapman. (2001, Walker Books Ltd).

Every effort has been made to trace copyright holders for the works reproduced in this book, and the publishers apologise for any inadvertent omissions.

Images

Page 28, Shadow puppets. © lynea/shutterstock.com

Author Donna Thomson

Editorial Rachel Morgan, Anna Hall, Kate Soar, Margaret Eaton

Consultants Hilarie Medler, Libby Allman

Cover and Series Design Neil Salt and Nicolle Thomas

Layout K & S Design

Illustration Gemma Hastilow-Smith

Cover Illustration Eddie Rego

Contents

How to use this book

- This book will help your child to practise and improve their skills in English.

- The content is divided into chapters that relate to different skills. The final 'Review' chapter contains a mix of questions that bring together all of these skills. These questions increase in difficulty as the chapter progresses.

- Keep the working time short and come back to an activity if your child finds it too difficult. Ask your child to note any areas of difficulty. Don't worry if your child does not 'get' a concept first time, as children learn at different rates and content is likely to be covered at different times throughout the school year.

- Find out more information about comprehension skills and check your child's answers at www.scholastic.co.uk/ses/comprehension.

- Give lots of encouragement and complete the 'How did you do' for each activity.

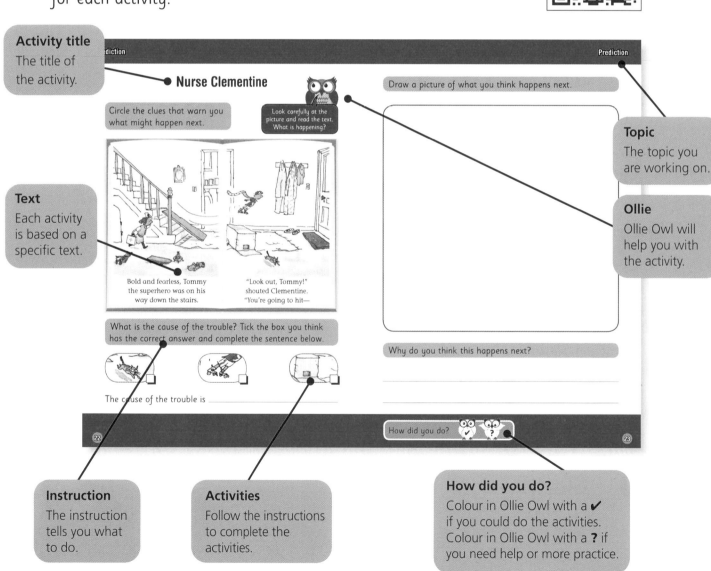

Activity title
The title of the activity.

Text
Each activity is based on a specific text.

Topic
The topic you are working on.

Ollie
Ollie Owl will help you with the activity.

Instruction
The instruction tells you what to do.

Activities
Follow the instructions to complete the activities.

How did you do?
Colour in Ollie Owl with a ✔ if you could do the activities. Colour in Ollie Owl with a **?** if you need help or more practice.

If you need help, ask an adult!

Character, action, place

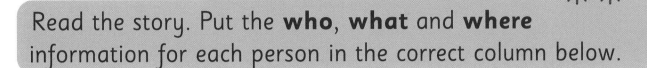

Who is in this story?
What are they doing? **Where** are they?

Read the story. Put the **who**, **what** and **where** information for each person in the correct column below.

Edith was reading her new book.

"What are you reading, Edith?" asked her little brother, Arthur.

"Go away, Arthur," said Edith.

Who is in the story?	**What** are they doing?	**Where** are they?

Read along the boxes to join the words into full sentences. Then retell what is happening using **who**, **what** and **where**.

Read, draw, retell

Read this sentence and underline the **who**, **what** and **where** words in different coloured pens.

Edith is reading to her pet rabbit in the garden.

Draw a picture of this sentence. Remember to include everything in the sentence.

Edith is reading to her pet rabbit in the garden.

Retell what is happening in the picture and text using **who**, **what** and **where** to help you.

How did you do?

What's the problem?

Read the story below. **Who** and **what** is it about?

The Storm Whale

As he got closer, Noi could not believe his eyes.

It was a little whale washed up on the sand.

What's the solution?

Discuss how the boy might solve the problem.
Then draw the solution in the box below.

Look at the picture below.

How did the boy solve the problem? Retell the story.

"I must be quick!" he thought.

How did you do?

How to make a paper dog face

Follow the instructions below to make a paper dog face.

First...	Next...
1. Fold the paper square in half.	**2.** Fold in half again to make a crease.
Then...	**Now...**
3. Fold in along the dotted line to make the ears.	**4.** Fold along the dotted line.
After that...	**Finally...**
5. Fold up to make the nose.	**6.** Draw a dog face.

Draw the instructions for making a paper dog face in the correct order below.

First...	Next...
Then...	**Now...**
After that...	**Finally...**

Now retell the instructions out loud. Make sure you get them in the correct order. Use your pictures and the labels to guide you.

How did you do?

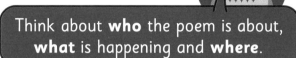

The Cat and the Bird

Read the poem aloud.

Think about **who** the poem is about, **what** is happening and **where**.

The Cat and the Bird

Black cat, hungry cat, creeping from his lair,

Blackbird, pulling worms, doesn't know he's there.

Black pup, waggy tail, looking for some fun –

Woof, woof, meow, meow – black cat's on the run!

Blackbird, you lucky bird – fly off far away.

Don't let that cat have bird for lunch today!

What do you think happens in the beginning, middle and end of the poem?

Beginning, middle, end

These pictures are not in order. Draw or write about the beginning, middle and end of the poem on page 11 in the empty boxes below.

Beginning: The story is about… (Who? What? Where?)	**Middle:** The problem is…
End: What happens in the end is…	

Retell what happens in the poem from the beginning to the end.

How did you do?

Bedtime story

Circle the characters in the picture and text.

Mum loves Granny's funny voices when she reads *Big Pig, Little Duck* to Joey and Lily.

Now write the questions for the answers below. The first has been done for you. Remember the question mark at the end.

Example:
Question: Who is pointing at the book?
Answer: Joey is pointing at the book.

Question: Who _____
Answer: Lily is cuddling a floppy duck.

Question: Who _____
Answer: Granny is reading *Big Pig, Little Duck*.

Question: Who _____
Answer: Mum loves Granny's funny voices.

How did you do?

Picnic

Circle the characters in the picture and text.

Duck, pig, sheep, boy and girl ran
as fast as they could towards
the wood to hide from bull.

Answer the question and then write your own **who** question and answer about the characters in the story.

Example:
Question: Who ran towards the wood?
Answer: Duck, pig, sheep, boy and girl ran towards the wood.

Question: Who was leading the group as they ran?
Answer: _____

Question: Who _____
Answer: _____

How did you do?

Dear Daddy

Circle what the characters are doing in the picture.

Answer the question below. Then write your own question and answer about **what** the characters are doing.

Question: What is Mum doing?

Answer: _____

Question: What _____

Answer: _____

How did you do?

The playground

Circle the characters and **what** they are doing in the text.

I am Reena. That's me kicking a football around with my cousin Kim and his friend on the grass. That's Kelly and her brother Rob playing on the swings. My friend Gabriel is climbing up a tree.

Write the answers to the questions.
Then ask and answer your own **what** question.

Question: What are Reena and Kim doing?
Answer: _____

Question: What are Kelly and Rob doing?
Answer: _____

Question: What _____ doing?
Answer: _____

How did you do?

Green Light for the Little Red Train

Circle the characters in the picture. Draw a line to the boxes below that describe **what** they are doing and **where**. One has been done for you.

Look at this scene. **What** is happening in the picture?

| on the sea | fishing | diving |

Duffy didn't realize they were under the sea!

| under the sea | travelling | in the sea |

Use the information below to help you answer the questions.

fishermen

on the sea

divers

in the sea

passengers

under the sea

Example:
Question: Where are the fishermen?
Answer: The fishermen are on the sea.

Question: Where are the divers?
Answer: _____

Question: Where are the passengers?
Answer: _____

Circle **where** the items in the list are in the picture.

Point to the sea, seabed and tunnel.

sailing boat

seal

octopus

shipwreck

engine driver

train

Now write your own **where** questions and answers about the people or things you have circled in the picture.

Example:
Question: Where is the train?
Answer: The train is in the tunnel under the sea.

Question: Where is _____

Answer: _____

Question: Where is _____

Answer: _____

How did you do?

Character, action, place

Circle the characters in the picture.

They went inside, so Iris could hide the lion properly. They had to be quiet, as mums and dads can be funny about having a lion in the house.

Underline the words below that tell you **who** the characters are (red pen), **what** they are doing (blue pen) and **where** they are (green pen).

Iris and the lion are climbing up the stairs.

Mum is reading the paper in her chair.

Dad is sleeping on the sofa.

The baby is awake in her basket.

Put the underlined **who**, **what** and w**here** information from page 20 in the correct column. The first one has been done for you.

Who	What (doing)	Where
Iris and the lion	are climbing up	the stairs

Use the information from the table above to write your own **who**, **what** and **where** questions and answers below.

Remember the question mark at the end of the questions.

Question: Who _____

Answer: _____

Question: What _____

Answer: _____

Question: Where _____

Answer: _____

How did you do?

Nurse Clementine

Circle the clues that warn you what might happen next.

Look carefully at the picture and read the text. What is happening?

Bold and fearless, Tommy the superhero was on his way down the stairs.

"Look out, Tommy!" shouted Clementine. "You're going to hit—

What is the cause of the trouble? Tick the box you think has the correct answer and complete the sentence below.

  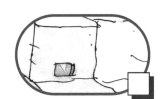

The cause of the trouble is _____

Draw a picture of what you think happens next.

Why do you think this happens next?

_____

_____

_____

How did you do?

Little Bo Peep

Read the nursery rhyme aloud. Then write the correct words from the box on the lines to complete the rhyme.

them	sheep	tails	home

Little Bo Peep has lost her _____,

And doesn't know where to find _____;

Leave them alone, and they'll come _____,

Bringing their _____ behind them.

Now read this different version of Little Bo Peep aloud. Underline the words that rhyme in each line.

Little Bo Peep has washed her sheep,

They'd got so grey and greasy,

But after a scrub

In a soapy tub

They came out white and fleecy.

How did you do?

Humpty and Bo Peep

The rhyme below is missing some words. Read the rhyme aloud. Then write the words from the box in the correct spaces.

Humpty Dumpty was very grumpy,

His shirt was tight and ever so _____.

His friend Bo Peep was _____ too,

Her shoes were odd – one brown, one blue.

They really didn't know what to _____!

Along came twins, Jack and Jill,

Huffing and puffing up the steep _____.

Jack's shirt was big enough for two,

Jill's shoes were odd – one brown, one _____.

What happened next? What did they do?

hill   lumpy   blue   do   fed up

What do you think happens next?

_____

_____

How did you do?

Book covers: fiction or non-fiction?

Look at the book covers below and read the titles.
Are the books **fiction** or **non-fiction**?
Tick the boxes and explain why below.

Book 1	**Book 2**

☐ Non-fiction   ☐ Non-fiction

☐ Fiction   ☐ Fiction

I think **Book 1** is non-fiction / fiction because _____

_____

I think **Book 2** is non-fiction / fiction because _____

_____

How did you do?

Creating a book cover

Look at the list of book titles. Write each title under the heading **fiction** or **non-fiction** in the table below.

My Town   How to Hide a Dinosaur   Hamsters

Lucy and the Magic Broom

Fiction	Non-fiction

Choose one of the titles above and draw your own cover. Then write what you think the book is about.

_____

_____

_____

_____

Shadow puppets

What do these symbols mean?

Write the animal names under the correct symbol.

camel (bear) wolf rabbit butterfly goat
dog elephant duck

bear
_____

_____

_____

_____

_____

_____

_____

_____

_____

How did you do?

The Three Little Pigs

Label each symbol using the correct words from the box.

farmer   straw   sticks   three little pigs   wolf

house of straw   house of bricks   house of sticks

1.  _____

2.  _____

3.  _____

4. _____

5.  _____

6.  _____

7.  _____

8.  _____

Retell the story using the symbols above to help you predict what happens. The first line has been given to you.

Once upon a time there were three little pigs...

How did you do?

Search for links

Can you link the smaller pictures to something in the main picture? Look carefully. One has been done for you.

fire

pets

cycling

spade

sun

shellfish

What is happening in the big picture on page 30?
Answer the questions below.

1. **What is the temperature like in the picture?**
   - ☐ It is a hot day.
   - ☐ It is a cold day.

2. **How do you know that?**
   - ☐ I know that because the boy is shivering.
   - ☐ I know that because a fire has been lit in the house.
     There is smoke coming from the chimney.

3. **Is the sun shining?**
   - ☐ Yes.
   - ☐ No.

4. **How do you know that?**
   - ☐ I know that because the scene in the picture looks
     dark and gloomy.
   - ☐ I know that because there are shadows on the sand.

5. **Does the family live by the sea?**
   - ☐ Yes, the family lives by the sea.
   - ☐ No, the family does not live by the sea.

6. **How do you know that?**

I know that because _____

_____

How did you do?

Sally and the Limpet

Circle the clues in the words and picture that suggest **who** and **what** the story is about and **where** it is happening. Think about how you know.

He heaved and groaned, but the limpet made a little squelching noise and held on even tighter.

The answers to detective questions can't be found right there in the text. You have to work them out using clues in the words and pictures.

Underline the clues in the questions to help you answer them. Then ask and answer your own detective question.

1. **What is Dad doing?**

   ❑ Dad is trying to get the limpet off Sally's finger.

   ❑ Dad is playing a game with Sally on the beach.

2. **How do you know that?**

   ❑ I know that because he is tugging hard at the limpet as he tries to pull it off her finger.

   ❑ I know that because they look like they are on holiday.

3. **Is it easy for Dad to get the limpet off Sally's finger? How do you know that?**

   _____

   _____

   Your detective question: _____

   _____

   Your answer: _____

   _____

How did you do?

Because...

Look at the pictures and sentences below. Write **because** in the space between the pictures.

Why does Tom love a windy day?

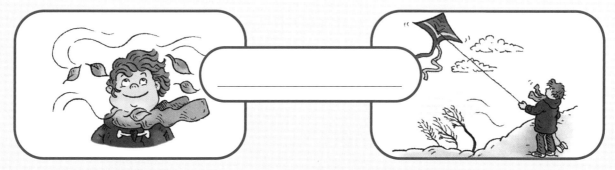

Answer: Tom loves a windy day **because** it means he can fly his kite.

Write a sentence using **because** to explain why Amy is shouting.

Why is Amy shouting?

Help!

Help, I can't get down!

Answer: _____

_____

How did you do?

Once There Was a Raindrop

Tick the correct answer below. Then write your answer using **because** to explain how you know.

Sometimes too much rain falls.

1. Why are the family standing on a platform under a tree?

   ☐ The family are standing on a platform under a tree because they are cold and wet.

   ☐ The family are standing on a platform under a tree because they are sheltering from the rain and trying to keep above the rising rain water.

2. What happens when too much rain falls? How do you know that?

   _____

   _____

How did you do?

Hugh Shampoo

Circle the clues in the words and the picture that suggest **what** the characters are doing and **where** they are.

Teacups tinkled, hairdryers hummed, and friends chatted, while Mr and Mrs Shampoo's scissors went snippety snip all day long.

Write the **word and picture clues** in the box below. Two have been done for you.

teacups	hairdryers

Answer the questions below using the **word and picture clues** to explain how you know. Then ask and answer your own inference question.

1. **Where are the characters?**

   ☐ The characters are at a friend's house for tea.

   ☐ The characters are in a hairdresser's salon.

2. **How do you know that?**

   ☐ I know that because they are friends and they are chatting and drinking tea together.

   ☐ I know that because one of the characters is having her hair cut and it says 'Mr and Mrs Shampoo's scissors went snippety snip all day long'.

3. **Is the scene busy and noisy? How do you know?**

   _____

   _____

   Your inference question: _____

   _____

   Your answer: _____

   _____

How did you do?

Hoppers

What do you think these playful objects are? Look for clues that suggest what they do.

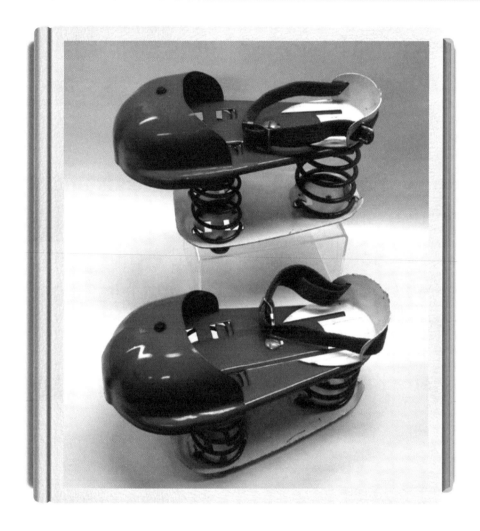

Some words in the box describe what 'hoppers' can do. Circle the words that make sense from the clues you have found.

| skate | jump | swim | sleep |
| slide | tiptoe | dance | spring |

Tick the correct boxes and answer the questions.

1. **Where would you wear hoppers?**

   ☐ on your hands   ☐ on your feet   ☐ on your head

2. **Why do you say that?**

   _____

   _____

3. **Why do you think they are called hoppers?**

   I think they are called hoppers because _____

   _____

4. **Why do you think they have straps and springs?**

   ☐   The straps measure the size of your feet and the springs help you to walk faster.

   ☐   The straps hold your feet in place and the springs help you to jump forwards and bounce up and down.

5. **What do you think the objects are?**

   ☐ skates   ☐ rollerblades   ☐ jumping shoes

6. **Why do you say that?**

   _____

   _____

How did you do?

Word web

Circle any words on the left that have a similar meaning to **jump**. Write them under the correct picture in the word web.

lift

leap

slide

spring

throw

bounce

dive

jump

Use these words to complete the passage below.

Ten tubby teddies on a trampoline,

Jump, teddy, jump! _____, teddy, _____!

Their coats are red and their hats are green,

_____, teddy, _____! _____, teddy, jump!

How did you do?

Zackary Dapp

The clues in the questions have similar meanings to the words in the rhyme.

Use the text to help you answer the questions below. Then write your own question and answer.

1. Who <u>began</u> to flap and <u>make the noise of a parrot</u>?

    ❑ The bird in the rhyme begins to flap and make the noise of a parrot.

    ❑ Zackary Dapp begins to flap and make the noise of a parrot.

Zackary Dapp
Started to flap,
Started to flutter and squawk,
Climbed on a chair,
Jumped in the air
And flew round the room like a hawk.

2. Does Zackary Dapp <u>leap</u> into the air? How do you know?

    _____

    _____

Your question (using a word with a similar meaning):

_____

Your answer: _____

How did you do?

Tadpole

Look at the pictures and read the words on the page.

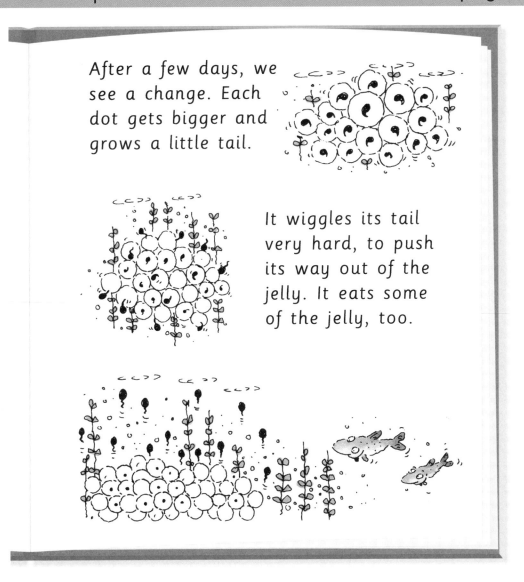

After a few days, we see a change. Each dot gets bigger and grows a little tail.

It wiggles its tail very hard, to push its way out of the jelly. It eats some of the jelly, too.

Skim and scan for these matching words in the text and underline them.

grows	wiggles	change	too	tail
few	dot	jelly	push	bigger

Remember, the answers are right there in the text.

Tick the correct boxes below and answer the questions. Use the words you have underlined on page 42 to help you.

1. **What happens when each <u>dot gets bigger</u>?**

   ☐ When each dot gets bigger it becomes a tadpole.

   ☐ When each dot gets bigger it grows a little tail.

   ☐ When each dot gets bigger it swims away.

2. **When can you see the <u>change happen to each dot</u>?**

   ☐ You can see the change happen after a few days.

   ☐ You can see the change happen as the dot gets bigger.

   ☐ You can see the change happen a little each day.

3. **What does it do to <u>push its way out of the jelly</u>?**

   _____

   _____

4. **What does it do with <u>some of the jelly</u>?**

   _____

   _____

How did you do? ✔ ?

How to Babysit a Grandad

Skim and scan the text and pictures. Circle the parts of the picture that match the underlined words in the text.

What other words would make sense instead of the underlined words in the text?

When you're back at home, have him shut his eyes while you get ready. And then . . .

HOW TO ENTERTAIN A GRANDAD:
- Somersault across the room
- Put on a scary play
- Show off your muscles.

You may want to have some extra tricks – grandads always clap for more.

Draw lines to match the words below.

Text words:

(entertain)

(somersault)

(scary)

(muscles)

Similar words:

(frightening)

(strength)

(head over heels)

(amuse)

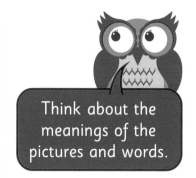

Underline the words in each question that link to **similar words** in the text. The first one has been done for you.

Answer the questions. Then ask and answer your own inference question.

Think about the meanings of the pictures and words.

1. Is the boy <u>putting on a show</u> for his grandad?
   How do you know that?

   ☐ No, the boy is not putting a show on for his grandad because he is just playing.

   ☐ Yes, the boy is putting on a show for his grandad because he is 'entertaining' his grandad.

2. Does the boy like acting and tumbling about?
   How do you know that?

   _____

   _____

   Your inference question: _____

   _____

   _____

   Your answer: _____

   _____

My Big Shouting Day

Circle the faces. Match the look on each face with the words beneath the picture. One has been done for you.

Look carefully at the scene and read the text. What is happening? How are the characters feeling?

And then we had to go shopping and Mummy said,
"Please stop wriggling, Bella."
But I couldn't stop wriggling and in the end I shouted:

Mummy said, "You will give Bob an earache. And you are giving *me* a headache."
And Bob poked me and said, "**ear**."

worried   cross   unhappy   amused

Tick the correct box and answer the questions.

1. **Why do you think Bella is shouting?**
    - ☐ I think Bella is shouting because she can't get out of the trolley and she feels too old to be in there.
    - ☐ I think Bella is shouting because she wants to stay in the trolley and Mum won't let her.

2. **How do you think everyone in the scene is feeling?**

    I think Mum is feeling **cross** because _____

    _____

    I think Bob is **amused** because _____

    _____

    I think the boy in the number 7 T-shirt is **unhappy** because

    _____

    I think the old lady passing by is feeling _____

    because _____

3. **How do you think the little girl with the long hair is feeling?**
    - ☐ Happy   ☐ Worried

    I think that because _____

    _____

How did you do?

We're Going on a Bear Hunt

Look at the first picture below. **Who** is in the picture? **What** are they doing? **Where** are they?

Look for the information on the page. Then search for clues that explain what is happening and how the characters are feeling.

Quick! Back through the cave! Tiptoe! Tiptoe! Tiptoe!

Look at the next picture. What do you think might happen?

Back through the snowstorm! Hoooo wooooo! Hoooo wooooo!

How do you think the characters are feeling and thinking in the picture below?

Back through the forest! Stumble trip! Stumble trip! Stumble trip!

Tick the correct box and answer the questions.

Think about the different question types.

1. **Where are the family in the first picture?**
   ☐ The family are by the seaside.
   ☐ The family are in a cave.
   ☐ The family are in a tunnel.

2. **Are the family returning the way they came? How do you know that?**

Yes, the family are returning the way they came. I know that

because _____

_____

_____

3. **Are the family enjoying their journey through the forest? Why do you think that?**

_____

_____

_____

4. **What do you think will happen in the end? Why do you think that?**

_____

_____

_____

How did you do? ✔ ?

My Busy Being Bella Day

Read the thoughts below. Can you match them with the characters in the picture? Write their thoughts in the bubbles.

I like that picture.

That's mine!

This is hard.

Oh dear!

This is fun.

Use the text and pictures on page 50 to help you answer the questions below. Then write your own evaluation question and answer.

What are the characters thinking and why?

1. Who do you think likes Erica's picture?

   ☐ Bella ☐ Sasha

   ☐ Joshua ☐ Erica

2. Why do you say that?

   I say that because _____

   _____

   _____

3. Do you think Bella is enjoying the activity? Why do you say that?

   _____

   _____

   _____

   Your evaluation question: _____

   _____

   Your answer: _____

   _____

Knuffle Bunny

Read the story below.

"Now, please don't get fussy," said her daddy.

Well, she had no choice...

Trixie bawled.

She went boneless.

Use the story on page 52 to help you answer the questions below. Then write your own evaluation question and answer.

What are the characters feeling and thinking?

1. **What do you think Dad means when he says 'please don't get fussy'?**
   - [ ] He means 'please don't be silent'.
   - [ ] He means 'please don't have a tantrum'.
   - [ ] He means 'please don't run away'.

2. **Why do you think the girl thinks she 'had no choice'?**
   I think the little girl thinks she 'had no choice' because

   _____

   _____

3. **Why do you think the little girl 'went boneless'?**

   _____

   _____

   Your evaluation question: _____

   _____

   _____

   Your answer: _____

   _____

How did you do? ✔ ?

We're Going on a Bear Hunt

Look for information in the picture below.

Tick the boxes next to the correct answers.

1. **Who is in the water?**

   ❑ Some children and a dog are in the water.

   ❑ A family and their dog are in the water.

2. **Why do you think they are in the river?**

   ❑ They need to get to the other side.

   ❑ They are chasing after their dog.

   ❑ They are washing themselves.

3. **What is Dad doing?**

   ❑ Dad is carrying the dog.

   ❑ Dad is carrying the baby.

4. **Why do you think Dad is doing that?**

   ❑ The baby is too little to be able to wade across.

   ❑ The baby is scared of the dog.

   ❑ The dog can't swim.

5. **Why do you think they are carrying their shoes?**

   ❑ They like to feel the mud between their toes.

   ❑ They don't want to get their shoes wet.

How did you do?

Newborn

Look for information in the picture.
Then answer the questions.

Tick the boxes next to the correct answers.

1. **Who is in the picture?**
    - ☐ A giraffe and three people are in the picture.
    - ☐ Two giraffes and three people are in the picture.

2. **What are the people in the picture doing?**
    - ☐ They are trying to move the giraffe.
    - ☐ They are measuring the height of the giraffe.

3. **How do you know that?**
    - ☐ They are holding the giraffe.
    - ☐ The man is using a tape measure.

4. **Is the giraffe a baby?**
    - ☐ No, the giraffe is not a baby
    - ☐ Yes, the giraffe is a baby.

5. **Why do you say that?**
    - ☐ The giraffe is taller than the people.
    - ☐ Giraffes are much taller than people but this one is only a little bit taller than the people.
    - ☐ The giraffe looks too big to be a baby.

How did you do?

Baby Brains

Read the story. Then answer the questions.

Mrs Brains opened the door to see her baby sitting on the sofa, reading the morning paper.

Tick the boxes next to the correct answers.
Write the answer to the final question on the lines.

1. **What is Mrs Brains' baby doing?**

   ☐ Mrs Brains' baby is on the floor in the sitting room.

   ☐ Mrs Brains' baby is sitting on the sofa
      reading the paper.

2. **Do you think Mrs Brains expected to see her baby when she opened the door? Why do you say that?**

   ☐ No, Mrs Brains did not expect to see her baby
      because she looks surprised to see him.

   ☐ Yes, Mrs Brains did expect to see her baby
      when she opened the door.

3. **Why do you think the author called the baby 'Baby Brains'?**

   ☐ The baby has an unusually large head.

   ☐ The word 'brains' can mean 'being clever'.

4. **Do you think Baby Brains is an unusual baby? Why do you say that?**

Yes, because _____

No, because _____

How did you do?

Tadpole

Read the text and look for information in the pictures.

Now the tadpole is changing quickly. First, its tail gets shorter. Its eyes start to bulge and its mouth gets wider.

Tick the box next to the correct answer to the first question. Write the answers to the other questions on the lines.

1. **What happens when the tadpole's tail gets shorter?**

☐ The tadpole gets bigger.

☐ The tadpole's eyes start to bulge and its mouth gets wider.

2. **Do the changes to a tadpole happen quickly? How do you know?**

_____

_____

3. **Which word in the text means 'begin'?**

_____

4. **What do you predict will happen next to the tadpoles? Why do you think that?**

_____

_____

_____

5. **Why do you think the children in the picture look surprised?**

_____

_____

How did you do?

Sally McDuff

Read the poem below.

Write answers to the questions on the lines.
Tick the correct answer to question 4.

1. Who are the children talking about in the poem?

_____

2. What is the problem?

_____

_____

3. Does Sally think snails are tastier than suet? How do you know that?

_____

4. What do you think suet is?

☐ flour   ☐ raisins   ☐ beef fat

5. Do you think the bugs, slugs and snails are Sally's pets? Why do you say that?

_____

_____

6. The boy says 'don't let her in'. What do you think will happen?

_____

_____

How did you do? ✔ ?

My Friend Nigel

Look at the picture and read the story.

Billy's dad and Billy's mum
Thought magic was a lot of fun.
You might think Bill would like it too
But quite the opposite was true.

Their spells were always going wrong
Mum's potions made a nasty pong.

Use the text and pictures on page 64 to help you answer the questions below.

1. **Whose spells are always going wrong?**

   ☐ Billy's spells   ☐ Mum and Dad's spells

2. **Does Billy think magic is a lot of fun?**

   ☐ No, Billy does not like magic spells.

   ☐ Yes, Billy loves magic spells.

3. **How do you know that?**

   _____

   _____

   _____

4. **Which of the words below has a similar meaning to the word 'potion' in the text?**

   ☐ mixture   ☐ face cream   ☐ cooking

5. **How do you think Billy feels when Mum and Dad's spells go wrong? Why do you say that?**

   _____

   _____

   _____

How did you do?

65

Traction Man and the Beach Odyssey

Read the story below.

Traction Man and Scrubbing Brush
are exploring the secret crevices of the Rockpool.

Traction Man is wearing his Squid-Proof Scuba Suit,
Lightweight Shorts and Aquatic Air Tanks.

Who knows what creatures lurk
in this Underwater World?

Tick the correct boxes or write the answers to the questions on the lines.

1. **What is the story about?**

   ☐ a day at the seaside

   ☐ an adventure under the sea

   ☐ sky-diving

2. **Who might be lurking underwater?**

   ☐ sea creatures

   ☐ Traction Man's friend

3. **Do you think Traction Man is able to breathe underwater? How do you know that?**

   _____

   _____

4. **Which sea creature does Traction Man's scuba suit protect him from? How do you know that?**

   _____

5. **The characters are exploring 'secret crevices' in the 'Rockpool'. What is a 'secret crevice'?**

   ☐ a spy   ☐ a hidden hole   ☐ a fish

Write your answers to the questions on the lines. Then write your own question and answer about the story.

6. Do you think the characters are going underwater for an adventure? Why do you think that?

_____

_____

_____

7. What do you think happens next in the story? Why do you say that?

_____

_____

_____

Your question: _____

_____

_____

Your answer: _____

_____

_____

How did you do?

One Tiny Turtle

Look for information on the page below.

She has come to eat crabs.
Millions swim up from deep water
to breed in the shallows.
Their shells crack as easily as
hens' eggs in her heavy jaws.
But in a week the feast is over
and Loggerhead disappears again.

15

Answer the questions below. Then write your own question and answer about the text on page 69.

1. Who comes to eat the crabs?

    ☐ a loggerhead   ☐ fish   ☐ hens

2. How many crabs swim up to the shallows?

    _____

3. What sort of creature do you think Loggerhead is? Why do you say that?

    _____

    _____

    _____

4. Do crabs have a problem when they swim up from deep water? How do you know that?

    _____

5. Why does Loggerhead find crabs easy to eat?

    _____

6. Why do you think Loggerhead leaves after a week of 'feasting'?

    _____

7. 'Their shells **crack** as easily as hens' eggs'. Think of another word for 'crack' here.

_____

8. Why do you think the author gave the book the title 'One Tiny Turtle'?

_____

_____

_____

9. Do you think Loggerhead is greedy and cruel? Why do you think that?

_____

_____

_____

Your question: _____

_____

_____

Your answer: _____

_____

_____

How did you do?

Well done!

Cut-out your reward Ollie.

Name:

....

You have completed

Comprehension

For ages 5-7

Age: ....

Date: ....